THE TENOR MANDOLA CHORD BIBLE

(CGDA Standard Tuning)

by

Tobe A. Richards

A Fretted Friends Publication for Cabot Books

Published by:
Cabot Books
Copyright © 2006 & 2016 by Cabot Books
All rights reserved.

First Edition February 2006
Second Edition February 2016

ISBN-13: 978-1-906207-24-3

No part of this publication may be reproduced in any form
or by any means without the prior consent of the publisher.

Cabot Books
3 Kenton Mews
Henleaze
Bristol
BS9 4LT
United Kingdom

Visit our online site at www.frettedfriendsmusic.com
e-mail: cabotbooks@blueyonder.co.uk

TABLE OF CONTENTS

Introduction..4-5

Fingering...5

Chord Theory & FAQs..6-7

Understanding Chord Boxes..8

Tenor Mandola Fingerboard & Tuning Layout..................9

Chords Covered in this Book...10

Slash Chords..11

Using a Capo or *Capo D'astra*......................................11

C Chords..12-16

C♯/D♭ Chords..17-21

D Chords...22-26

D♯/E♭ Chords..27-31

E Chords...32-36

F Chords...37-41

F♯/G♭ Chords..42-46

G Chords...47-51

G♯/A♭ Chords..52-56

A Chords...57-61

A♯/B♭ Chords..62-66

B Chords...67-71

Major Slash Chords...72-75

A Selection of Moveable Chord Shapes...................76-79

The Mandolin Family Factfile & Tunings..................80-82

Alternative Chord Name Chart.......................................83

Notes..84-86

Chord Window Blanks..87-110

INTRODUCTION

The Tenor Mandola Chord Bible provides the musician with 1,728 chords in all keys, featuring 68 different chord types, with 3 variations of each standard chord. 144 major slash chords are also included, together with 48 moveable chord shape diagrams (providing access to a further 576 barré and standard moveable chords) making this the most comprehensive reference guide for the Tenor mandola currently available. For many years now, guitarists have been able to pick up a songbook and instantly play the songs in front of them, either with the help of one of the many published guides, or through the chord boxes supplied with most popular music. With the help of this *Chord Bible*, beginners and experienced Tenor mandola players alike will be able to take advantage of the many songbooks, fake books and musical compendiums by any artist you would care to name, from *The Beatles* to *Joan Baez*, from *Planxty* to *The Pogues* or *Springsteen* to *Simon & Garfunkel*. With 68 different chordal variations in all keys, virtually any song should be playable!

Having a good chordal knowledge should arguably be the bedrock in any fretted or keyboard musicians armoury. Whether you're playing rock, pop, folk, jazz, blues, country or other types of music, it's impossible to supply a suitable accompaniment to any vocal or solo instrumental music without providing a chordal or harmonic backing. The subtle nuance of an added ninth chord over a major chord is something that can't be captured simply by playing a melody line. In theory it is possible to approximate the harmonic intervals of any music using a limited palette of chords - probably around ten to twelve. But wherever possible it's best to use correct harmonies if they're available to you.

Having four courses of strings, the tenor mandola is obviously limited to four note chords, but by making acceptable compromises and omitting the least important parts of that chord, even the most complex musical structures are possible. For instance, in the case of an eleventh, the third is generally omitted without the character of the chord being adversely affected. Equally, the root or key note isn't always necessary to achieve an effective approximation of the full chord. The third is rarely missing from the majority of chords (other than elevenths) as it determines whether the key is major or minor - although this isn't a hard and fast rule, particularly in folk music where the root and fifth form the basis of most traditional music. These two intervals are generally the starting point for a number of open tunings of instruments as diverse as the guitar, the Irish bouzouki and the mountain dulcimer. The same interval is also used in a lot of heavy rock where a fifth chord is described as a *power chord*. Even though a power chord is technically neither major nor minor, it's more often used as an alternative for a major chord in most popular music.

One question which often pops up is *how many chords do I need to learn?* The smart answer is '*how long is a piece of string?*', which is true, but it doesn't actually answer the question if you don't know where to start. My advice would be to begin with simple chord clusters like the popular G, C, D and Em progression and gradually work in new ones as you advance. If you intend playing within a rock format, it's probably sensible to learn the E, A, B sequence which is the staple of most guitarists and bassists. As a generalisation, jazz probably requires the greatest chordal knowledge of any form of music, so the learning curve will be longer if you're planning to pick up any songbook and instantly produce a recognisable version of your favourite *Duke Ellington* or *Steely Dan* number. The only truth as far as harmonic knowledge goes is you can never learn *too* much!

In this series of chord theory books, I've included a comprehensive selection of configurations of chords in all keys. As I mentioned previously, this will enable you to pick up virtually any songbook or fake book (topline melody and chord symbols) and look up the chord shape that's needed. Obviously, you'll come across the occasional song which doesn't conform to the normal harmonic intervals which you find in this, or any other chord theory publication, but with a little experimentation and experience, you'll be able to make a reasonable stab at it. For instance, most players would be more than a little bemused if they suddenly came across an instruction to play a *Gbmaj7add6/D*. Fortunately, this is fairly unusual, but from the knowledge you'll have learned, you'll be able to use a similar chord or work it out note by note. Put simply, if *every* theoretically possible chord shape were to be included in this or any other book, the result would resemble something akin to several volumes of the *Yellow Pages*!

FINGERING

Always a tricky subject and one which seems to generate a lot of discussion and differing opinions as to which method is correct. Personally, I take the view that it's a largely fruitless exercise, as the number of variables involved make a definitive answer unlikely. So what I've decided to do in this book is to choose fingering positions which feel comfortable to me. Some chord shapes will dictate the fingering used, but others will be down to personal preference. If you can practise your two and three finger chords using different fingers, it will make your playing a lot more fluid when you change to another chord shape. But if you develop habits which limit you to one playing position, it isn't the end of the world either, if you can make the transitions seamless.

The only rules, if you could loosely call them that, are:-

a) Don't abandon using your pinky or little finger if you're just beginning to play, as you'll eventually need it for some of the four finger chords which frequently crop up.

b) Try to avoid fretting with the thumb unless you're learning an instrument like the mountain dulcimer which requires a longer stretch. I know a number of players employ it on slimmer necked instruments, but I personally feel it leads to bad habits.

c) Keep your left hand fingernails short or fretting becomes a major problem. Obviously do the reverse if you're a lefty.

d) If you're a beginner and you're naturally left handed, don't get persuaded into buying a right handed instrument - it won't work! The learning curve will be steeper and you'll never get the fluidity you'd achieve with your natural hand. Most acoustic instruments can be adapted for a left hander apart from cutaway guitars and f-style mandolins etc., by reversing the nut and strings. For the non-reversible instruments, always go for a left handed model.

e) Learn to barré with other fingers apart from your index finger. This will prove invaluable with more complex chords and increase finger strength as well.

f) Don't be afraid to use fingerings further up the neck in combination with open strings as these will give you interesting new voicings and are generally quite popular in folk music. A number of these are provided in this book.

g) The tenor mandola can be played with a pick or fingerpicks. Alternatively, fingernails can be used if you're accustomed to this method of playing. Using a pick or fingerpicks generally produces a brighter sound with more attack.

CHORD THEORY & FAQs

Q *What is a chord?*
A It's a collection of three or more notes played simultaneously. The exceptions in this book are the fourths and fifths (power chords) which aren't in the strictest sense, true chords. For convenience sake, they are classed as such.

Q *What is a triad?*
A A chord containing three notes. For example, G Major, Bm, D+ or Asus4.

Q *What are intervals?*
A Intervals are the musical distance between notes in a musical scale. For instance in the scale of C Major, C is the 1st note, D is the 2nd note, E the 3rd and so on. So if you're playing the chord of C Major, your intervals will be 1–3–5 or C as the *first* note, E as the *third* note and G as the *perfect fifth*.

Q *What is a chromatic scale and which intervals does it contain?*
A: A chromatic scale encompasses all twelve notes in a musical scale, including the sharps and flats. It's also the basis for the naming of *every* chord in existence. See the staff diagram below to see the intervals:

Chromatic Scale in C

Root or 1st | Minor 2nd | Major 2nd | Minor 3rd | Major 3rd | Perfect 4th | Augmented *or* Diminished 4th / 5th | Perfect 5th | Minor 6th | Major 6th | Minor 7th | Major 7th

Q *What is a seventh chord?*
A: In its most basic form, an additional note beyond the triad. Sevenths can be either major or flattened. For instance, returning to our old friend, the key of C, a *Cmaj7* has an added *B* on top of the *C–E–G* triad. The resultant chord has a mellow quality often found in jazz. Now if you take the B and flatten it by dropping the fourth note in your chord down to a B flat, you get a C7.

Q: *Then why isn't it called a C minor seventh?*
A: Technically this *is* a minor seventh note, but this would create a lot of confusion when naming chords, as you already have a minor interval option in your triad (in the key of C major, E flat), so it's always referred to as a 7th to differentiate between it and a major seventh.

Q: *What is an extension?*
A: A chord which goes beyond the scope of triads and sevenths. Basically, extensions are additional notes placed above the triad or seventh in a musical stave, fingerboard or keyboard. It's important to understand these are, for theoretical purposes, always placed above the seventh. Or in layman's terms, higher up the scale. The confusion comes when you start to realise a 9th is identical to a 2nd - in the scale of C – a D note.

Q: *So why is the ninth note the same as the second note?*
A: This takes a little grasping, but if you remember that if your note goes higher than the seventh it's a 9th, but if it's lower, it'll be a 2nd. An example of this would be Csus2, which contains the root

note of C, a 2nd or suspended D note and a G, the perfect 5th. You'll see this even more clearly if you look at the piano keyboard diagram below. Count from the C up to the following D beyond the 7th (B note). From the C to the second D is exactly nine whole notes.

Q: *Do any other extensions share a common note?*
A: Yes, other examples include the *11th*, which is also a *4th* and the *13th* which shares a note with the *6th*.

Q: *What are inversions?*
A: In the root version of a chord, the notes run in their correct order from lowest to highest. In the case of G major, it would be G–B–D. With an inversion of the same chord the notes would run in a different order. For example, the first inversion of G major would be B–D–G and the second, D–G–B. In general, triads sound more or less the same when they're inverted, but that's certainly not the case with sevenths and extensions which can sound quite different and occasionally discordant when the notes are jumbled up in certain configurations. Inversions can also produce different chords using the same basic notes. A good example of this would be *C6 (C-E-G-A)* which produces an *Am7 (A-C-E-G)* when it's inverted (both contain the notes of C–E–G–A, but in a different order). The major variations are in the tonal properties of the chords, making them sound quite different from one another.

Q: *Do elevenths and thirteenths have any particular properties?*
A: Yes. In most cases the 3rd is omitted from eleventh chords and the 11th from the majority of thirteenths as they're deemed unnecessary and arguably, create unwanted dissonance.

Q: *Some chords are called by different names in different music books. What should I do?*
A: The alternative chord name reference chart at the back of the book should help sort out the confusion.

Q: *What is a suspended chord?*
A: It's simpler to think of suspended chords as a stepping stone to a major or resolving chord. In effect the third has been left in a state of suspension by either raising it to a fourth (sus4) or lowering it to a second (sus2). Sevenths also provide versions of the suspended chord in the form of C7sus4 or C7sus2 (using the key of C as an example).

Q: *What is a diminished chord?*
A: A diminished chord has a dissonent quality to it where the third and fifth notes in a triad are flattened by a semi-tone. Again, using C as an example, C major (C-E-G) is altered to Cdim (C-E♭-G♭). A second version of a dimished chord is also used in many forms of music, the diminished seventh. This retains the elements of a standard diminished chord, adding a double flat in the seventh (C-E♭-G♭-B♭♭). A B♭♭ in this case is, to all intents and purposes, really an A note.

Q: *What is an augmented chord?*
A: An augmented chord basically performs the opposite task to a diminished one. Instead of lowering the fifth by a semitone, it raises it by the same interval. A C+ (augmented) chord contains the triad of C-E-G♯. The major root and third are retained and the fifth is sharpened.

UNDERSTANDING THE CHORD BOXES

The three diagrams below show the chord conventions illustrated in this guide. Most experienced fretted instrument players should be familiar with them. The suggested fingering positions are only meant as a general guide and will depend, in many instances, on hand size, finger length and flexibility, so feel free to experiment. The location of the black circles is unalterable, though, if you want to produce the correct voicing.

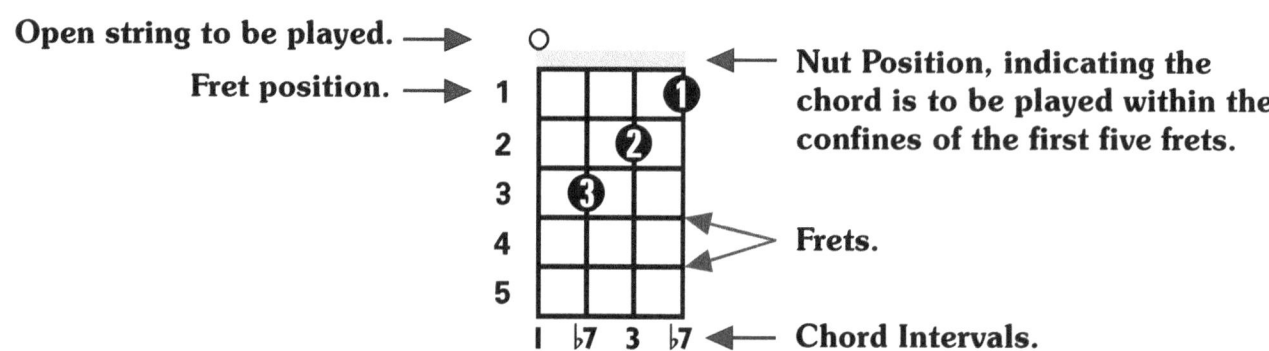

Open string to be played.

Fret position.

Nut Position, indicating the chord is to be played within the confines of the first five frets.

Frets.

Chord Intervals.

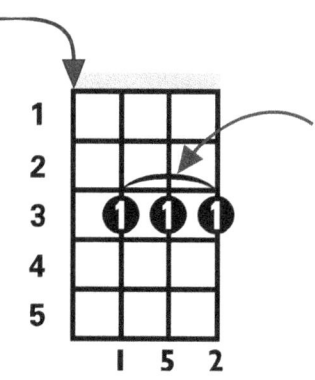

If there are no markers above or below the string, the string should not be played.

Barré chord (in this example, a three string barré to be fretted with the index finger).

Suggested fingering. In this case the 1st or index finger marker is displayed.

A damped string. In this example the 3rd string should be damped using the lower pad of the middle finger, fretting the 4th string.

A two string barré to be played with the fourth finger.

Left to right: 4th, 3rd, 2nd and 1st courses of strings.

Whether a fretted instrument has single strings or pairs of strings, the chord boxes in this book, other chord dictionaries and songbooks treat it as a four stringed instrument. This convention is common to all double or triple course instruments such as the mandolin or tiple, making the diagrams a lot less confusing and free from unnecessary clutter.

TENOR MANDOLA
FINGERBOARD & TUNING LAYOUT

Fingerboard note layout

All matched pairs

Mandola Tuning in Standard Notation

Note:
With notation based on standard viola tuning, the alto clef can be used instead of the treble clef illustrated above.

To tune your tenor mandola accurately, it's best to use an electronic chromatic tuner, but if there isn't one available, you can tune it to a guitar or piano/electronic keyboard. The following tuning grid gives the correct fingering positions on the guitar fingerboard and piano keyboard.

Tenor Mandola	Guitar	Piano
1st & 2nd strings (A)	1st string (E) fretted at the 5th fret	1st A above middle C
3rd & 4th strings (D)	2nd string (B) fretted at the 3rd fret	1st D above middle C
5th & 6th strings (G)	3rd open string (G)	1st G below middle C
7th & 8th strings (C)	5th string (A) fretted at the 3rd fret	1st C below middle C

THE CHORDS COVERED IN THIS BOOK

Chord	Chord Name in Full	Harmonic Interval
C	Major	1–3–5
Cm	Minor	1–F3–5
C-5	Major Diminished Fifth	1–3–F5
C°	Diminished	1–F3–-F5
C4	Fourth	1–4
C5	Fifth or Power Chord	1–5
Csus2	Suspended Second	1–2–5
Csus4	Suspended Fourth	1–4–5
Csus4add9	Suspended Fourth Added Ninth	1–4–5–9
C+	Augmented	1–3–S5
C6	Major Sixth	1–3–5–6
Cadd9	Major Added Ninth	1–3–5–9
Cadd11	Major Added Eleventh	1–3–5–11
Cm6	Minor Sixth	1–F3–5–6
Cm-6	Minor Diminished Sixth	1–F3–5–F6
Cmadd9	Minor Added Ninth	1–F3–5–9
C6add9	Major Sixth Added Ninth	1–3–5–6–9
Cm6add9	Minor Sixth Added Ninth	1–F3–5–6–9
C°7	Diminished Seventh	1–F3–F5–DF7
C7	Seventh	1–3–5–F7
C7sus2	Seventh Suspended Second	1–2–5–F7
C7sus4	Seventh Suspended Fourth	1–4–5–F7
C7-5	Seventh Diminished Fifth	1–3–F5–F7
C7+5	Seventh Augmented Fifth	1–3–S5–F7
C7-9	Seventh Minor Ninth	1–3–5–F7–F9
C7+9	Seventh Augmented Ninth	1–3–5–F7–S9
C7-5-9	Seventh Diminished Fifth Minor Ninth	1–3–F5–F7–F9
C7-5+9	Seventh Diminished Fifth Augmented Ninth	1–3–F5–F7–S9
C7+5-9	Seventh Augmented Fifth Minor Ninth	1–3–S5–F7–F9
C7+5+9	Seventh Augmented Fifth Augmented Ninth	1–3–S5–F7–S9
C7add11	Seventh Added Eleventh	1–3–5–F7–11
C7+11	Seventh Augmented Eleventh	1–3–5–F7–S11
C7add13	Seventh Added Thirteenth	1–3–5–F7–13
Cm7	Minor Seventh	1–F3–5–F7
Cm7-5	Minor Seventh Diminished Fifth	1–F3–F5–F7
Cm7-5-9	Minor Seventh Diminished Fifth Minor Ninth	1–F3–F5–F7–F9
Cm7-9	Minor Seventh Minor Ninth	1–F3–5–F7–F9
Cm7add11	Minor Seventh Added Eleventh	1–F3–5–F7–11
Cm(maj7)	Minor Major Seventh	1–F3–5–7
Cmaj7	Major Seventh	1–3–5–7
Cmaj7-5	Major Seventh Diminished Fifth	1–3–F5–7
Cmaj7+5	Major Seventh Augmented Fifth	1–3–S5–7
Cmaj7+11	Major Seventh Augmented Eleventh	1–3–5–7–S11
C9	Ninth	1–3–5–F7–9
C9sus4	Ninth Suspended Fourth	1–4–5–F7–9
C9-5	Ninth Diminished Fifth	1–3–F5–F7–9
C9+5	Ninth Augmented Fifth	1–3–S5–F7–9
C9+11	Ninth Augmented Eleventh	1–3–5–F7–9–S11
Cm9	Minor Ninth	1–F3–5–F7–9

Chord	Chord Name in Full	Harmonic Interval
Cm9-5	Minor Ninth Diminished Fifth	1–F3–F5–F7–9
Cm(maj9)	Minor Major Ninth	1–F3–5–7–9
Cmaj9	Major Ninth	1–3–5–7–9
Cmaj9-5	Major Ninth Diminished Fifth	1–3–F5–7–9
Cmaj9+5	Major Ninth Augmented Fifth	1–3–S5–7–9
Cmaj9add6	Major Ninth Added Sixth	1–3–5–6–7–9
Cmaj9+11	Major Ninth Augmented Eleventh	1–3–5–7–9–S11
C11	Eleventh	1–3–5–F7–9–11
C11-9	Eleventh Diminished Ninth	1–3–5–F7–F9–11
Cm11	Minor Eleventh	1–F3–5–F7–9–11
Cmaj11	Major Eleventh	1–3–5–7–9–11
C13	Thirteenth	1–3–5–F7–9–11–13
C13sus4	Thirteenth Suspended Fourth	1–4–5–F7–9–11–13
C13-5-9	Thirteenth Diminished Fifth Minor Ninth	1–3–F5–F7–F9–11–13
C13-9	Thirteenth Minor Ninth	1–3–5–F7–F9–11–13
C13+9	Thirteenth Augmented Ninth	1–3–5–F7–S9–11–13
C13+11	Thirteenth Augmented Eleventh	1–3–5–F7–9–S11–13
Cm13	Minor Thirteenth	1–F3–5–F7–9–11–13
Cmaj13	Major Thirteenth	1–3–5–7–9–11–13

Key: F = Flat   S = Sharp   DF = Double Flat

SLASH CHORDS

What is a slash chord? Put simply, they're standard chords with an added note in the bass. *So what differentiates a C chord from a C/G when the G is already part of that chord, in this case, the fifth?* Theoretically, nothing, but the difference is very apparent when you actually sound the chord. The G bass is emphasised to provide a different feel to the harmonics. Slashes are also commonly found when the music calls for a descending bassline. For example; C, C/B, C/A and C/G.

The note after the slash indicates the bass note being played. For instance C/D would be an instruction to play a C chord with a D bass.

Slash Note. Generally found on the 4th & 3rd courses.

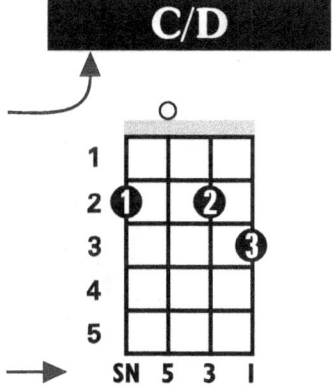

How do I play a slash chord that isn't listed in this book? Well, firstly, it would be an almost impossible task to cover every possible slash chord in existence, because the variations are potentially even greater than with standard chords. What you can do, within the confines of this guide, is to find the part of the chord before the slash in the main body of the book and then look for the nearest bass note on the third or fourth course of strings. To find the right bass note, consult the fingerboard layout on *page 9*.

USING A CAPO (OR *CAPO D'ASTRA*)

Using a capo is a quick and easy way of changing key to suit a different vocal range or to join in with with other musicians playing in a different key. For the uniniated, a capo is a moveable bar that clamps onto the fingerboard of fretted instruments. It works in much the same way as using a finger barré to hold down the strings. They come in a variety of designs and prices, the simplest using a metal rod covered in rubber and sprung with elastic. For the tenor mandola look for a mandolin or tenor banjo capo.

C Chords

C	Cm	C7	Cm7

C5	C6	Cm6	Cmaj7

C Chords

C°	C°7	C-5	C+

Csus2	Csus4	C7sus4	Cm7-5

C Chords

Cadd9

Cmadd9

C6add9

Cm6add9

C7-5

C7+5

C7-9

C7+9

C Chords

Cm(maj7)

Cmaj7-5

Cmaj7+5

C9

Cm9

Cmaj9

C11

C13

C Chords (Advanced)

C#/D♭ Chords

D♭	D♭m	D♭7	D♭m7

D♭5	D♭6	D♭m6	D♭maj7

C#/ D♭ Chords

D♭°	D♭°7	D♭-5	D♭+

D♭sus2	D♭sus4	D♭7sus4	D♭m7-5

C#/ D♭ Chords

D♭add9

D♭madd9

D♭6add9

D♭m6add9

D♭7-5

D♭7+5

D♭7-9

D♭7+9

C#/D♭ Chords

D♭m(maj7)

D♭maj7-5

D♭maj7+5

D♭9

D♭m9

D♭maj9

D♭11

D♭13

C#/ D♭ Chords (Advanced)

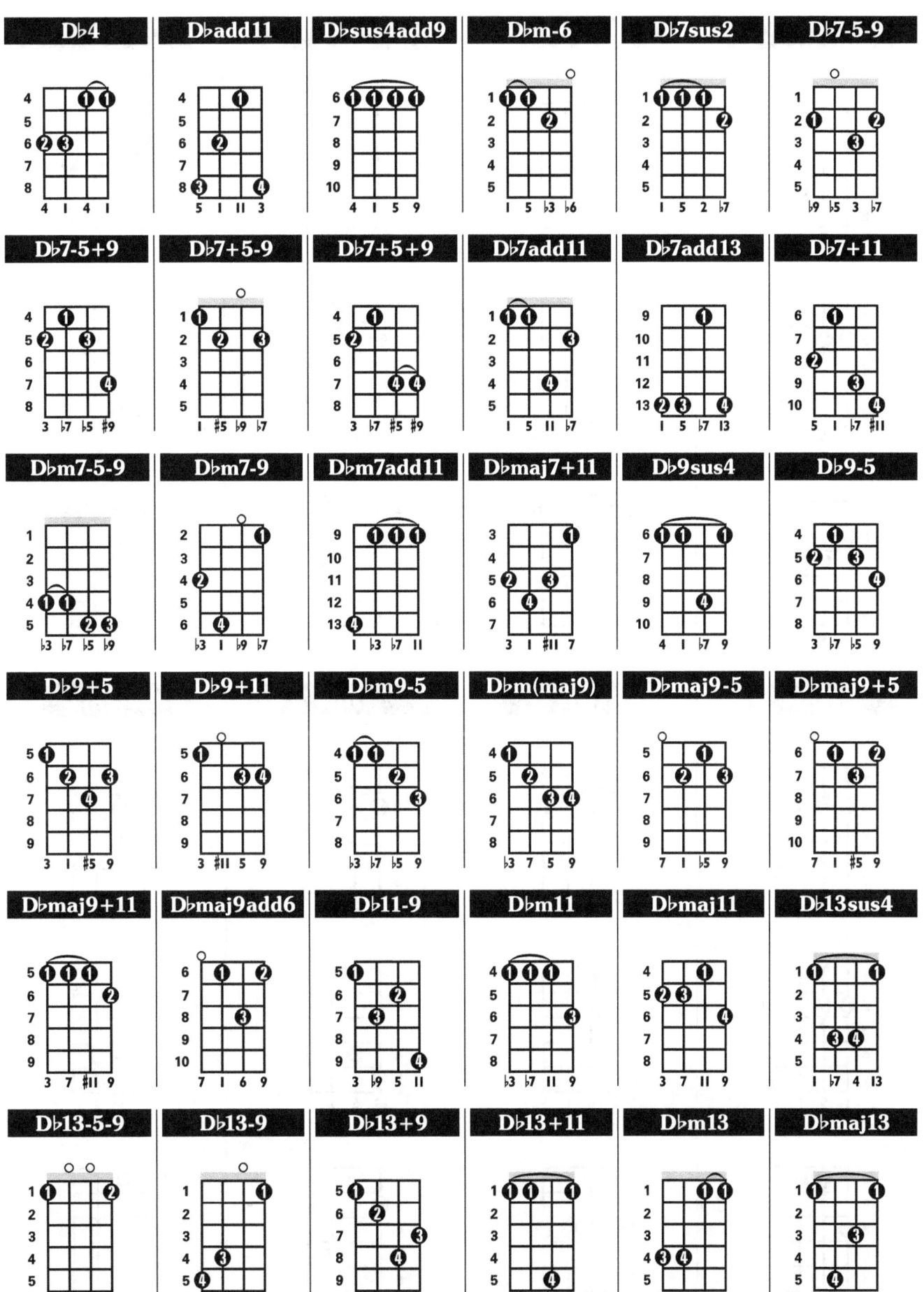

D Chords

D	Dm	D7	Dm7

D5	D6	Dm6	Dmaj7

D Chords

D°

D°7

D-5

D+

Dsus2

Dsus4

D7sus4

Dm7-5

D Chords

Dadd9	Dmadd9	D6add9	Dm6add9

D7-5	D7+5	D7-9	D7+9

D Chords

Dm(maj7)

Dmaj7-5

Dmaj7+5

D9

Dm9

Dmaj9

D11

D13

D Chords (Advanced)

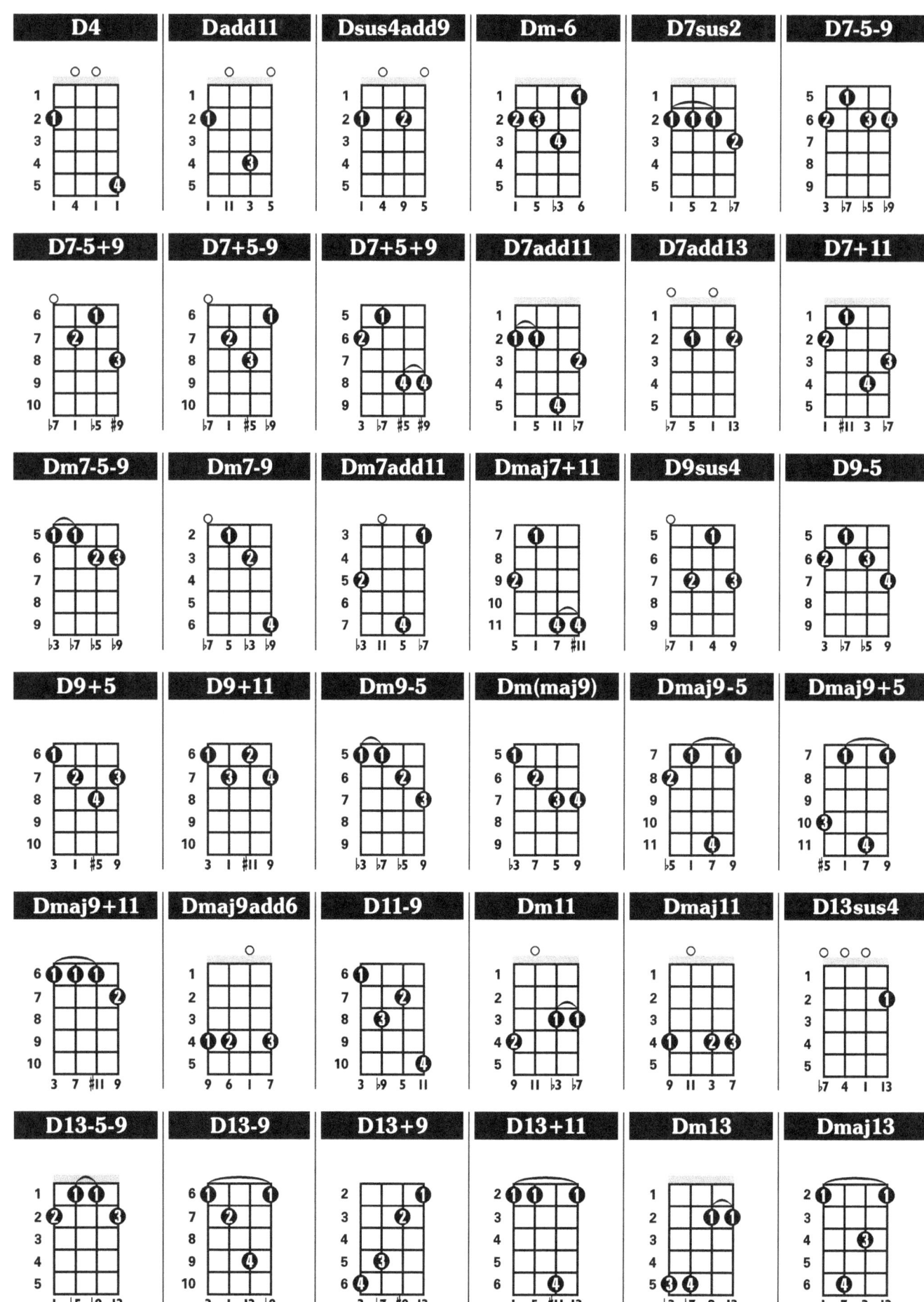

D♯/ E♭ Chords

E♭

E♭m

E♭7

E♭m7

E♭5

E♭6

E♭m6

E♭maj7

D#/ E♭ Chords

E♭°	E♭°7	E♭-5	E♭+

E♭sus2	E♭sus4	E♭7sus4	E♭m7-5

D#/ E♭ Chords

E♭add9

E♭madd9

E♭6add9

E♭m6add9

E♭7-5

E♭7+5

E♭7-9

E♭7+9

D#/ E♭ Chords

E♭m(maj7)	E♭maj7-5	E♭maj7+5	E♭9

E♭m9	E♭maj9	E♭11	E♭13

D#/E♭ Chords (Advanced)

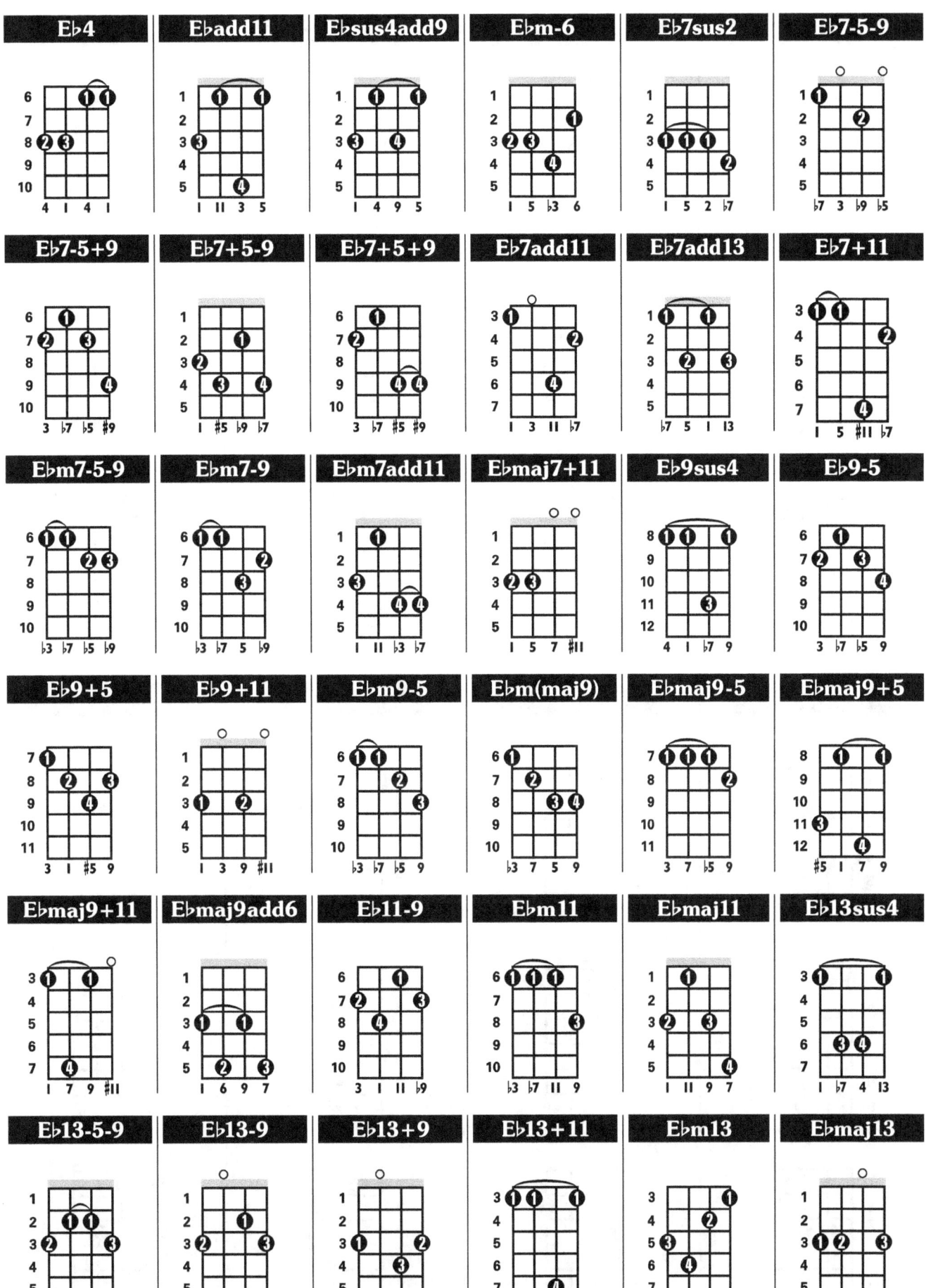

E Chords

E	Em	E7	Em7

E5	E6	Em6	Emaj7

E Chords

E°	E°7	E-5	E+

Esus2	Esus4	E7sus4	Em7-5

E Chords

Eadd9	Emadd9	E6add9	Em6add9

E7-5	E7+5	E7-9	E7+9

E Chords

Em(maj7)

Emaj7-5

Emaj7+5

E9

Em9

Emaj9

E11

E13

E Chords (Advanced)

F Chords

F

Fm

F7

Fm7

F5

F6

Fm6

Fmaj7

F Chords

F Chords

Fadd9

Fmadd9

F6add9

Fm6add9

F7-5

F7+5

F7-9

F7+9

F Chords

Fm(maj7)

Fmaj7-5

Fmaj7+5

F9

Fm9

Fmaj9

F11

F13

F Chords (Advanced)

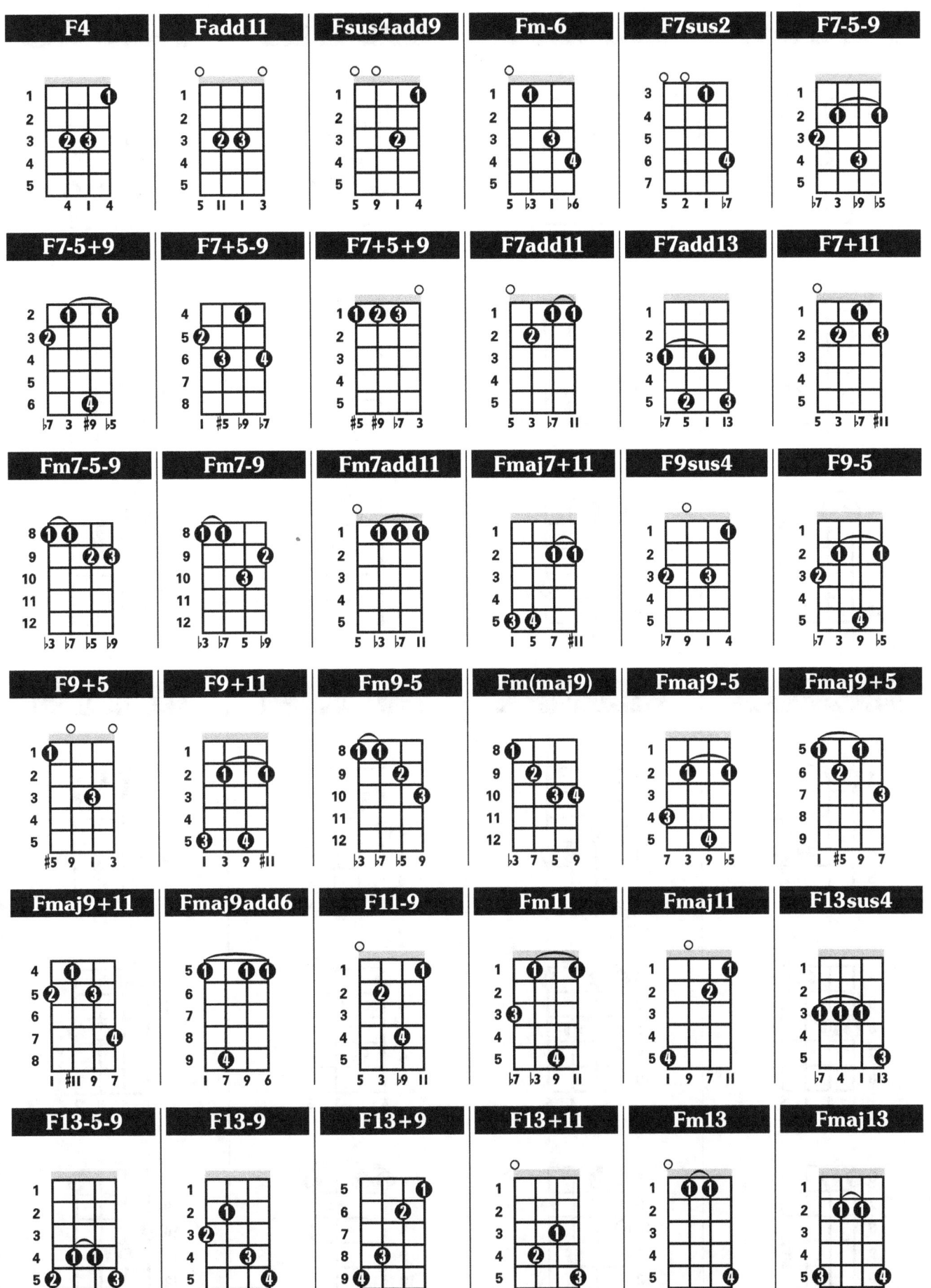

F#/G♭ Chords

F#	F#m	F#7	F#m7

F#5	F#6	F#m6	F#maj7

F#/G♭ Chords

F#°	F#°7	F#-5	F#+

F#sus2	F#sus4	F#7sus4	F#m7-5

F#/G♭ Chords

F#add9

F#madd9

F#6add9

F#m6add9

F#7-5

F#7+5

F#7-9

F#7+9

F#/G♭ Chords

F#m(maj7)

F#maj7-5

F#maj7+5

F#9

F#m9

F#maj9

F#11

F#13

F#/ Gb Chords (Advanced)

G Chords

G

Gm

G7

Gm7

G5

G6

Gm6

Gmaj7

G Chords

G°	G°7	G-5	G+

Gsus2	Gsus4	G7sus4	Gm7-5

G Chords

Gadd9

Gmadd9

G6add9

Gm6add9

G7-5

G7+5

G7-9

G7+9

G Chords

Gm(maj7)	Gmaj7-5	Gmaj7+5	G9

Gm9	Gmaj9	G11	G13

G Chords (Advanced)

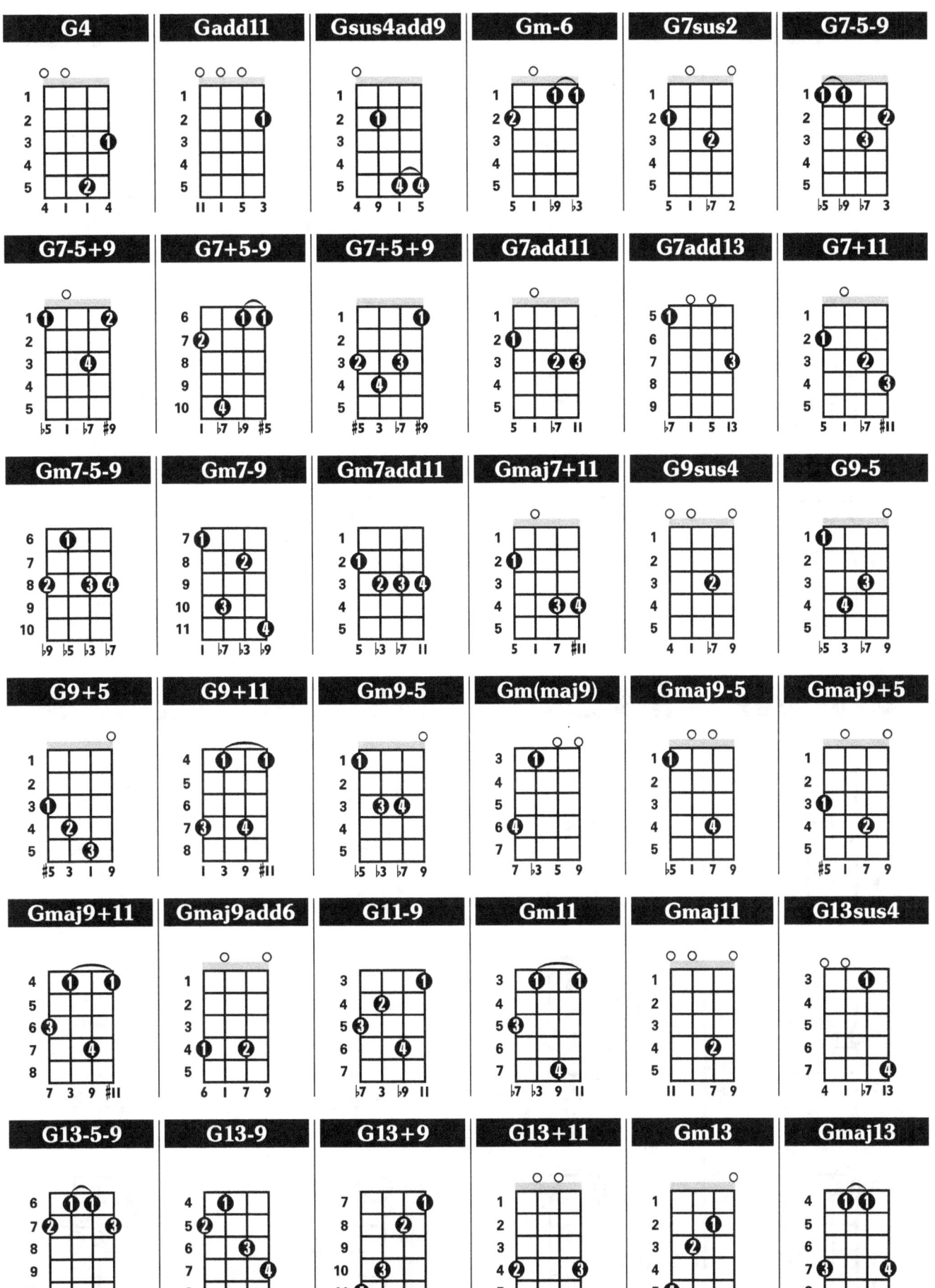

G♯ / A♭ Chords

A♭

A♭m

A♭7

A♭m7

A♭5

A♭6

A♭m6

A♭maj7

G#/A♭ Chords

A♭°

A♭°7

A♭-5

A♭+

A♭sus2

A♭sus4

A♭7sus4

A♭m7-5

G♯ / A♭ Chords

A♭add9	A♭madd9	A♭6add9	A♭m6add9

A♭7-5	A♭7+5	A♭7-9	A♭7+9

G#/A♭ Chords

A♭m(maj7)

A♭maj7-5

A♭maj7+5

A♭9

A♭m9

A♭maj9

A♭11

A♭13

G# / A♭ Chords (Advanced)

A Chords

A	Am	A7	Am7

A5	A6	Am6	Amaj7

A Chords

A°	A°7	A-5	A+

Asus2	Asus4	A7sus4	Am7-5

A Chords

Aadd9

Amadd9

A6add9

Am6add9

A7-5

A7+5

A7-9

A7+9

A Chords

Am(maj7)

Amaj7-5

Amaj7+5

A9

Am9

Amaj9

A11

A13

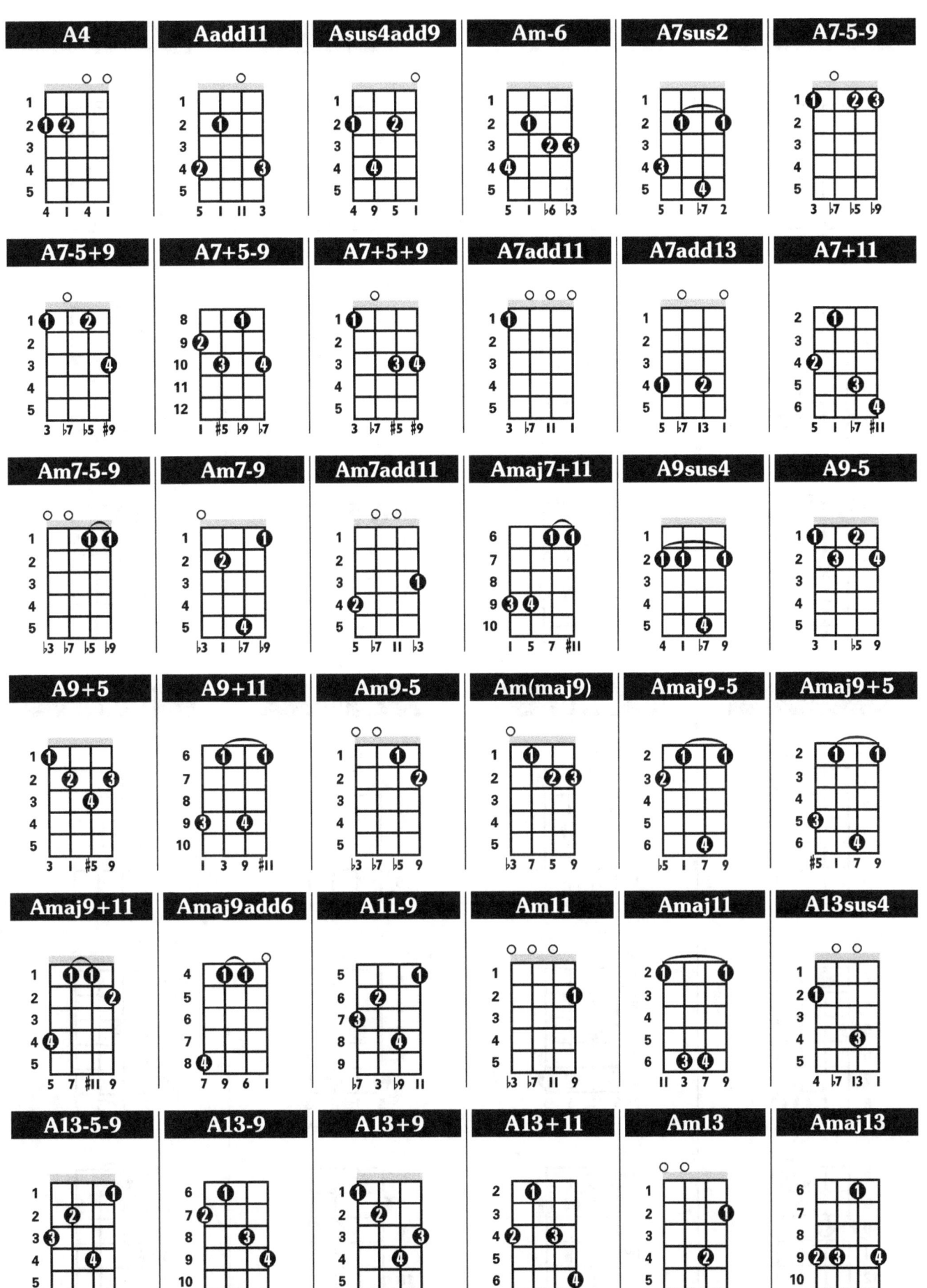

A♯ / B♭ Chords

B♭

B♭m

B♭7

B♭m7

B♭5

B♭6

B♭m6

B♭maj7

A#/B♭ Chords

B♭°

B♭°7

B♭-5

B♭+

B♭sus2

B♭sus4

B♭7sus4

B♭m7-5

A♯ / B♭ Chords

B♭add9	B♭madd9	B♭6add9	B♭m6add9

B♭7-5	B♭7+5	B♭7-9	B♭7+9

A#/B♭ Chords

B♭m(maj7)

B♭maj7-5

B♭maj7+5

B♭9

B♭m9

B♭maj9

B♭11

B♭13

A# / B♭ Chords (Advanced)

B Chords

B

Bm

B7

Bm7

B5

B6

Bm6

Bmaj7

B Chords

B°

B°7

B-5

B+

Bsus2

Bsus4

B7sus4

Bm7-5

B Chords

Badd9

Bmadd9

B6add9

Bm6add9

B7-5

B7+5

B7-9

B7+9

B Chords

Bm(maj7)

Bmaj7-5

Bmaj7+5

B9

Bm9

Bmaj9

B11

B13

B Chords (Advanced)

Major Slash Chords

Major Slash Chords

Major Slash Chords

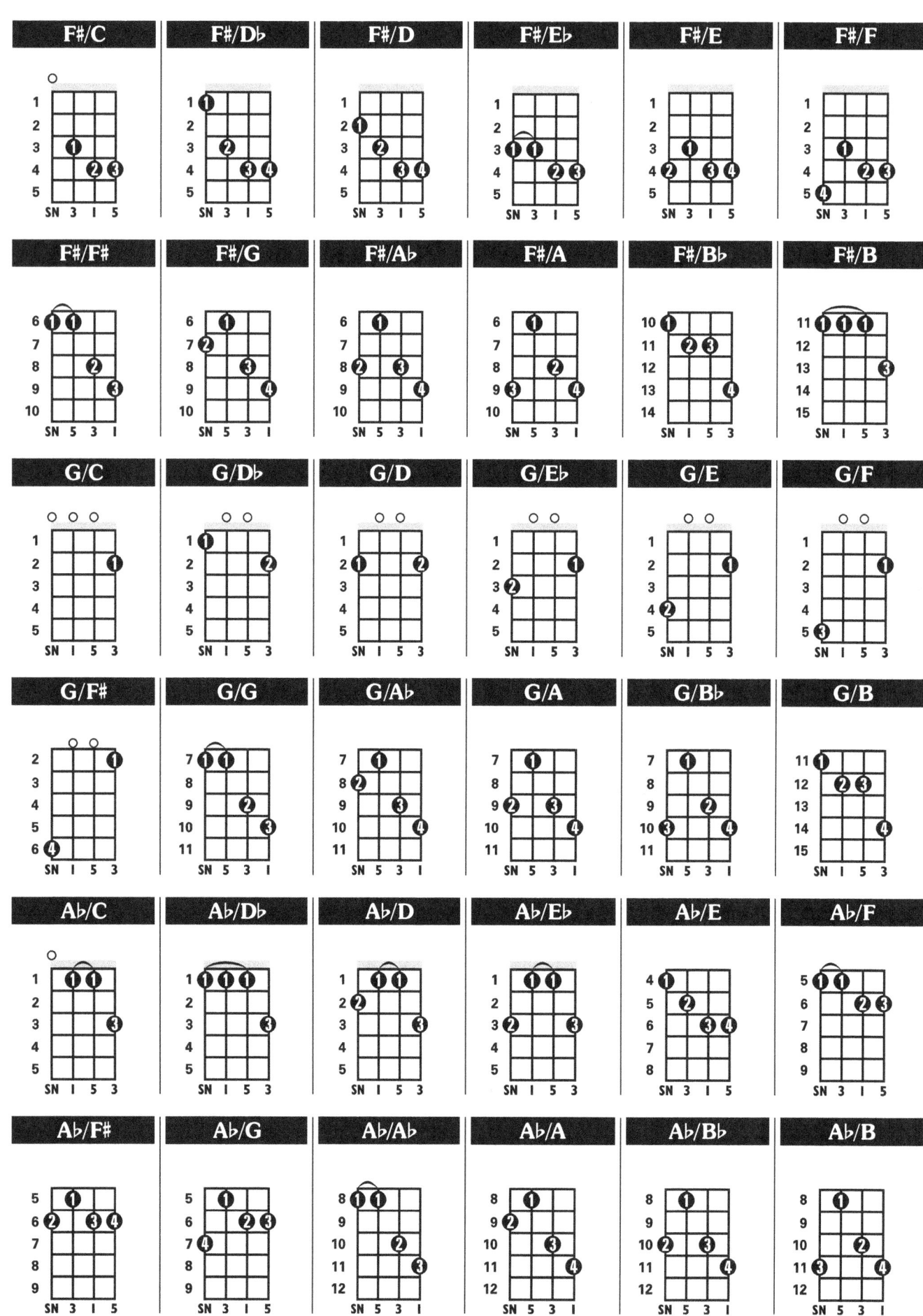

74

Major Slash Chords

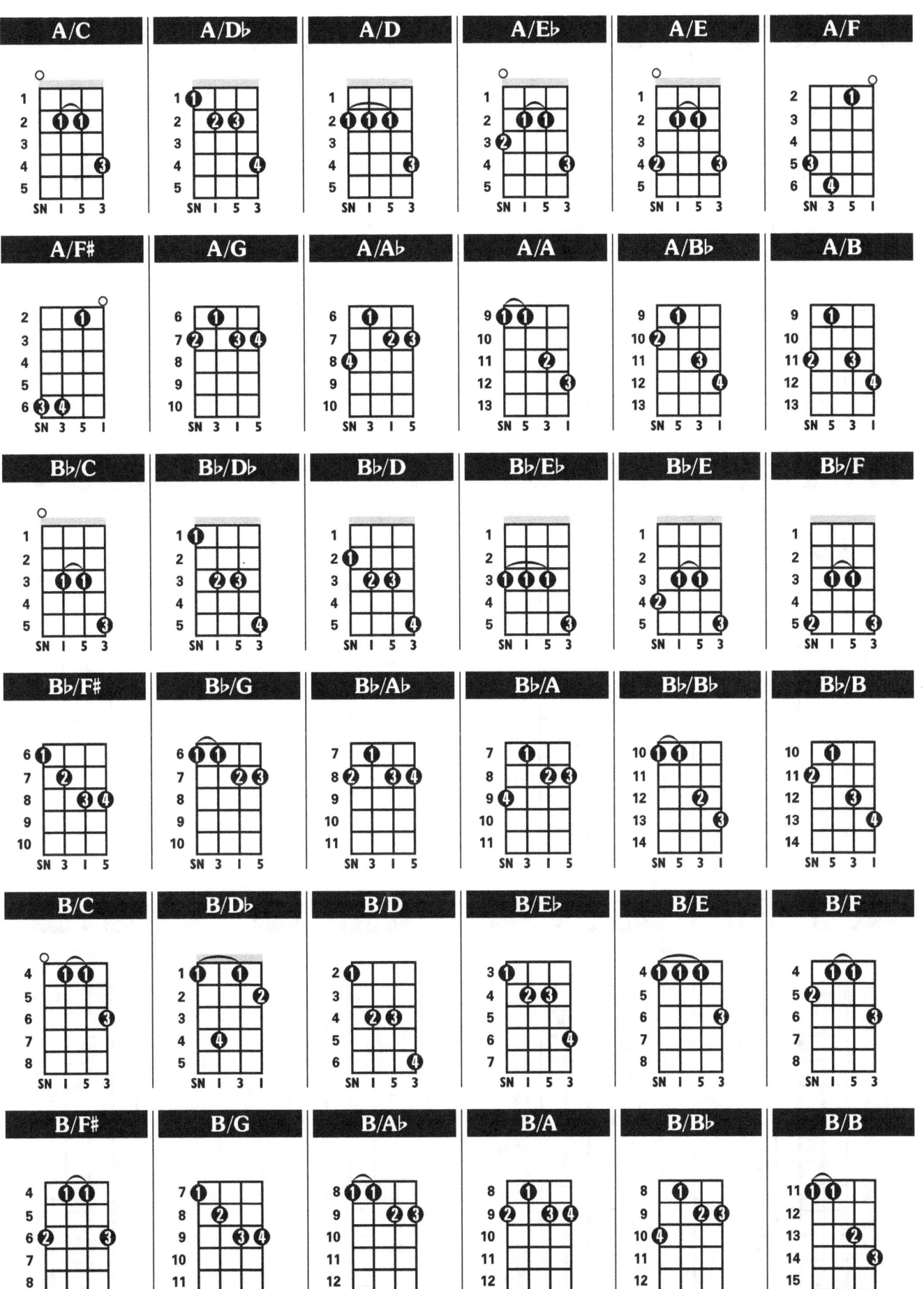

75

A Selection of Moveable Chord Shapes

A Selection of Moveable Chord Shapes

Minor Seventh

Sixth

Minor Sixth

A Selection of Moveable Chord Shapes

Major Seventh

Major Seventh

Major Seventh

Suspended Fourth

Suspended Fourth

Suspended Fourth

Diminished

Diminished

Diminished

Augmented

Augmented

Augmented

A Selection of Moveable Chord Shapes

MANDOLIN FAMILY FACTFILE

Andylin
A specially designed long scale mandolin commissioned by Andy Irvine. The new instrument was christened by luthier Davy Stuart of New Zealand and is pitched a whole tone lower than standard mandolin tuning with a dropped first course (FCGC).

Baglama *or* Greek Baglama
Visually, the little Greek Baglama resembles a scaled down version of the trichordo bouzouki with its generally ornate inlaid face and ribbed bowl back. Like it's big brother, the trichordo, the baglama is tuned modally to D-A-D, but pitched an octave higher. The stringing arrangement features unison pairs on the 4 highest strings and an octave pair on the lower D. Musically, the Baglama is most often found in the *Pireas* style of Rembetika, where it takes on the accompaniment role of supporting the bouzouki.

Physically, the little baglama resembles a half size bouzouki with its often intricate inlaid face and bowl back. Where it differs is in the construction of the body, which is generally made from a hollowed out piece of wood or gourd. The neck and head used to be made from one piece of wood, but today tend to be constructed separately. Its small size made it particularly popular with musicians who needed an instrument tranportable enough to carry around easily or small enough to conceal under a coat - a useful plus point for rembetes who found themselves locked up in jail for varying offences (a not uncommon occurance!).

Bandolim
Portuguese version of the mandolin. The bandolim features Preston-style tuners and a flatback, but still retains the standard GDAE tuning of its Italian counterpart. The teardrop shape is also more akin to the modern cittern-style instrument family, rather than the traditional Italian design of the bowl-back mandolin.

Cittern *or* Celtic Cittern
The modern celtic-style flatback cittern generally has five courses of strings and a variety of scale lengths of anything between 530mm/21 inches and 650mm/25½ inches. Confusingly, these are referred to as citterns by some luthiers and 5-string bouzoukis by others. Ultimately though, the nomenclature used by the different makers matters less than the scale length they employ on their particular instruments.

Of all the members of the mandolin/cittern family, the 10-course instrument has the least established standardized tuning, with players experimenting with various modal and mandolin-style configurations. Current popular tunings include: CGDAE, DGDAD, DGDAE, DGDGD, DADAD and EAEAE for long scales and GDADA, GDAEB, GDAEA, GCGCG, ADADA and ADGAD for short scales. Although the edges do get a little blurred when referring to scale lengths, as a rough guide, long scales can be up to 650mm/25½ and short scales between 530mm/21 and 580mm/23 inches. String selection also plays an important part in determining this as well.

English Guittar *or* English Guitar
The term English guittar is actually something of a misnomer. This 6-course, 10-stringed instrument should more accurately be classed as a form of cittern. It's popularity ran from the 1750s up until the 19th century where it was used as a parlour-style instrument. The only instruments you're likely to see today are luthier built reproduction models or antique instruments which have been restored. The tuning of the English guitar is set to a C major chord (C-E-G-C-E-G).

Arguably, the most famous maker of English guittars was John Preston of London whose watch-key style tuners can still be seen in operation today in instruments such as the Portuguese guitar and German waldzither. The waldzither in particular needs a special tuning wrench to tighten up or loosen the strings on the headstock. Musicians will generally wind their own strings for this style of instrument with a special string winder built for this purpose.

Greek Bouzouki *or* Bouzouki
The roots of the bouzouki can allegedly be traced way back to ancient Greece in the form of an instrument called a *pandouris* or *pandourion*. Like the modern trichord bouzouki it had three courses of strings and is claimed to be the very first lute-like fretted instrument. The documentation on this forerunner of the bouzouki is a little sketchy, but a carving of a pandouris can be seen on an artifact called the *Mantineia Marble*. The scene depicts a contest between Apollo and Marsyas, watched over by a muse sitting on a rock playing the pandouris.

Moving a little further forward in history to the Byzantine era, musicians were playing a very similar long necked lute called a tambouras. An instrument which to all intents and purposes is the equivalent of the modern Turkish tanbur. An example of this can be seen at the *National Historical Museum of Greece*. The instrument belonged to a military hero called General Makriyiannis.

A direct descendant of the modern bouzouki is probably an instrument of the saz family called a *bozouk saz*. The rough translation of the word bozouk means broken. A term which is said to refer to its size in comparison with other types of saz, rather than its state of repair! An alternative etymological basis of the word bozouk refers to the different tunings and scales (or *düzen*, in Turkish) employed by musicians in the region. A direct example of this can still be found in Greek folk music, called *bozouk duzeni* (or broken tuning).

Historically, the journey taken by the bouzouki from Turkey to Greece probably begins with the 1919-1922 war in Asia Minor, where ethnic Greeks were forced to flee across the border into mainland Greece. The newly patriated Greeks included musicians who brought a style of music with them called *Smyrneika*, which at the time was played on the oud (or Arabic lute). From these modern origins, the oud was dispensed with in favour of the more dynamic 3-course bouzouki and Smyrneika gradually evolved into the popular *Rembetika* (or Greek blues) that we know today.

Construction-wise, the bouzouki body (or *skalfi*) is pear or teardrop shaped with the rounded bowl back built from individual staves of shaped wood. The soundhole is generally oval shaped, although it's not uncommon for more decorative designs to be used as well.

Well known exponents of the Greek bouzouki include: Markos Vamvakaris, Yiorgos Batis, Vassilis Tsitsanis, Manolis Chiotis etc.

Halszither
A five-course guitar-shaped Swiss instrument that gained popularity at the end of the 19th and the start of the 20th century. The direct translation of halszither is 'cittern with a neck', to differentiate it from a standard tabletop zither. There are two dinstinct designs, the most popular being the Krienser named after the region in Switzerland where it was made. The second, the Toggenburger halszither conformed to more of standard cittern shape and featured 13 strings in 6 courses. Today, the halszither is very much a speciality instrument made to order by experienced luthiers.

If you are lucky enough to come across one, it's likely to be the Krienser model and not the Toggenburger which all but disappeared by the turn of the last century. Tuning for the Krienser is generally GDGBD (or open G Major) and CGCEG (or open C Major) for the Toggenburger.

Harzzither *or* Bergzither
The harzzither was a German cittern-style instrument, not dissimilar to its close relative, the waldzither. It was named after the Harz Mountain range in central Germany where it was made by local luthiers, who were very often musicians themselves. The stringing arrangement conforms more to the mandolin family than to it's cousin, the waldzither, with 8 strings set out in 4 courses. The tuning was GCEG (or open C Major). Traditionally, the harzzither is played with a plectrum to accompany a singer or as part of a folk music orchestra.

Irish Bouzouki
The history of the Irish bouzouki is relatively short in relation to other members of the mandolin family. It can be traced back to 1966 when Johnny Moynihan returned from a holiday in Greece with a traditional Greek bouzouki. He retuned it and began using it at gigs, despite intital scepticism from fellow musicians and audience alike. The potential of this unusual instrument

must have struck a chord at some point as Moynihan's bandmate, Andy Irvine, started using it as well, in *Sweeney's Men*. Irvine in turn gave Dónal Lunny a bouzouki and the *Planxty* sound was born. Other Irish folk outfits gradually cottoned on to the unique qualities of the zouk, including Boys of the Lough, De Danann and The Bothy Band and through further exposure in America and Europe, the instrument began to get a foothold in traditional music. Today the bouzouki is well established in all styles of folk music and has begun making inroads into other musical genres including bluegrass, jazz and rock. The established tunings for the Irish bouzouki are GDAD, GDAE and ADAD.

The first 'true' Irish bouzouki was created by guitar luthier, John Bailey, for Johnny Moynihan, who dispensed with the ribbed bowl back found on Greek instruments and opted for a flatback design instead. Then in 1970, the English luthier, Peter Abnett worked with Donal Lunny to produce the first example of the bouzouki design we see today. Significantly he called this instrument an *Irish bouzouki*. Another leading innovator during the evolution of the Irish zouk is British luthier, Stefan Sobell who based his designs on the shape of a Portuguese guitarra along with the acoustic qualities of the Martin C-3 guitar. A further divergence along the bouzouki design route brought the lower pitched bass bouzouki commissioned by Andy Irvine from luthier Davy Stuart. This shares the same harmonic relationship with the standard Irish zouk, but is tuned a fourth lower (DAEA). A typical scale length is generally between 560-610mm or 22-24 inches.

Laúd and Bandurria
A pair of Spanish folk instruments related to the mandolin/cittern family featuring a configuration of 12 strings in 6 courses tuned in 4ths. The laúd is tuned exactly one octave below its little sibling, with both forming an integral part of a traditional Spanish musical ensemble, together with the classical guitar. Because of its very short scale length, the bandurria tends to rely on melody playing, while its big brother, the laúd is more suitable for chodal work. Standard tuning for both instruments is G#-C#-F#-B-E-A. Several other family members of this group exist, but the bandurria and laud are by far the most widely used in today's Spanish folk music.

Mandobass
A very rare beast, even in its hey-day when Gibson produced these leviathans of the mandolin family as a direct replacement for the double bass. The tuning, like the upright or electric bass, is EADG.

Mandocello
As the name suggests, the mandocello takes its name and tuning from another member of the violin family, the cello. The tuning is pitched one octave below that of the mandola (CGDA), although it's not uncommon to string the instrument with lighter gauge strings and tune it like an Irish bouzouki or octave mandolin/mandola. In theory it's possible to tune down an Irish bouzouki or octave mandolin to CGDA, but the additional strain on the neck and body can cause structural problems. The heavier strings can also cause rattling in the lower courses. The mandocello has a scale length of between 630-660mm or 24¾-26 inches.

Mandola *or* Tenor Mandola
The mandola, as it's known in North America or tenor mandola in the United Kingdom, Ireland and Europe, takes its tuning directly from the viola (CGDA). It's also referred to in some circles as the alto mandola, reflecting the musical difference between it and the higher pitched *soprano* mandolin which is tuned GDAE (or a fifth higher). The scale length of a typical mandola is approximately 420mm or 16½ inches. Like other members of the mandolin family, the mandola is most popularly used within the many strands of European and North American folk music.

Mandolin
The mandolin comes in a bewildering array of different styles and constructional configurations, with the only constant being its traditional GDAE tuning in fifths. Its antecedents can be traced back as far as 15,000 B.C. and can be seen in its earliest forms in cave paintings. A typical mandolin has a scale of between 330mm and 370mm or 13-14½ inches.

The Neopolitan round or bowl-back style is mainly used in the classical repetoire. The bowl-back style we know today, though, can more accurately be attributed to the Italian Vinaccia family of luthiers from Naples. An existing example from 1744 of the family's work can be seen at the Conservatoire Royal de Musique in Brussels. Another fine example is on display at London's Victoria & Albert Museum. Although less common than other styles of mando, the Neopolitan is still popular today.

The F-Style or Florentine style mando was originally designed and built by New York born Orville H. Gibson. In 1902 a group of businessmen bought Gibson's patent and set themselves up as the Gibson Mandolin-Guitar Company. Gibson himself was originally employed as a consultant, gaining partnership status in 1915. The F-style is easily recognizable by its ornamental body scroll and violin-style f holes. Although not exclusively so, its popularity lies in bluegrass music where the sound is able to cut through and compete with other larger bodied instruments like the guitar and banjo.

The pear-shaped A-Style again is a Gibson design and can be found in a variety of music including folk, classical and bluegrass. It generally doesn't have quite the projection of the F-style, but has remained one of the popular standard designs to this day.

Celtic flatbacks are primarily used in folk music because of their rich tone, volume and sustaining qualities. They generally come with oval or round soundholes and make an ideal companion for other instruments such as the guitar and Irish bouzouki. Because of their long sustain, they're not really suitable for bluegrass music which requires a quick attack and rapidly decaying 'chop' sound.

Electric solid body and semi-acoustic mandolins are also common today. These have found their way into rock and other styles of music and come in single or double course versions. 5-String electric and acoustic mandolins are also becoming popular because of the additional lower course and are generally tuned CGDAE.

Octave Mandolin *or* Octave Mandola
The naming conventions on both sides of the Atlantic differ in much the same way as with the mandola or tenor mandola, with the term octave mandolin being used in North America and octave mandola in the UK, Ireland and Europe. As the name implies, the octave mandolin is pitched exactly one octave below the standard mandolin. The scale length can vary quite a bit from 500mm up to something as long as 600mm (19¾ to 23½ inches).

Piccolo *or* Sopranino Mandolin
A specialist instrument tuned exactly one octave above the mandola (CGDA) and only available from independent luthiers. The scale length is around 240mm or 9½ inches. As with other members of the mandolin family, the piccolo mando was created as a direct musical relation of the piccolo or sopranino violin.

Portuguese Guitar *or* Guitarra Portuguesa
The Portuguese guitar is a 12-string double course instrument used mainly within the confines of *Fado* music. The instrument's historical links can be traced back to the English Guittar and the Renaissance cittern, although there is still considerable debate about the specific parentage. This heritage was very apparent up until the end of the World War II, when the Portuguese guitar employed the same C-E-G-C-E-G *Natural* tuning as its English ancestor. Today, this has all but died out, with musician's opting for the current regional tunings associated with the two models of guitarra.

On the design front, there are two distinct designs with their own traditional regional tunings. Firstly, the Coimbra with its teardrop headstock protuberance and 470-490mm scale length tuned C-G-A-D-G-A. Secondly, the Lisboa or Lisbon guitarra, featuring a violin-like scroll on the headstock, a narrower neck/fingerboard arrangement and a shorter scale length of 440 or 458mm. The instrument is pitched D-A-B-E-A-B and is particularly associated with the accompaniment of *Fado* singing. Both forms include octave strings on the lowest three courses. Sound-wise, the Coimbra guitar has a fuller timbre with more bass response, while the Lisboa has more of a ringing tone. Different shaped *unhas* or finger and thumb picks are also employed by the two instruments. The Coimbra being rounded at the top like a fingertip as opposed to the Lisboa's much squarer corners, each producing its own very distinct sound and associated technique.

<u>Simple Pronunciation Guide:</u>
Coimbra: *Queem-brah*
Lisboa: *leezh-boa (with a soft 'g' sound on the 's')*
Unha (singular) / Unhas (plural): *oon-yah / oon-yas*

Traditionally, a picking technique called *dedillo* (or *dedilho*) is employed by musicians utilising only the index finger and thumb.

Tambura, Tamburitza *or* Tamburica

A family of instruments found in Bosnia, Herzegovina, Croatia, and Serbia frequently played in groups of three to ten people. Large orchestras featuring this group of instruments also exist, which are capable of tackling the most complicated pieces from the classical repetoire. The group consists of the following family members:

Samica: *6 strings in 3 courses.*
Bisernica: *4 strings (doubled) and 2 single strings in 4 courses.*
Prim: *1 double string and 3 single strings in 4 courses.*
Brač *or* Basprim: *4 strings (doubled) and 2 single strings in 4 courses.*
Čelović: *4 strings (doubled) and 2 single strings in 4 courses.*
Čelo: *4 single strings in 4 courses.*
Bugarija *or* Kontra: *4 strings (doubled) and 1 single string in 3 courses.*
Berda, Bas *or* Begeš: *4 single strings in 4 courses.*

Tricordia *or* Mandriola

A triple course mandolin from Mexico (tricordia) and Europe (mandriola). The difference between the two being the use of octave strings in the European instrument as opposed to the tricordias unison pairings. The sound is a lot fuller than the standard double-course mandolin with more of a shimmering timbre to it.

Tzouras *or* Tsouras

The tzouras could loosely be described as the missing link between the bouzouki and the baglama. Length-wise it resembles a bouzouki, but features a much smaller body, which again is constructed along the same lines as the little baglama. The body can be a one piece affair carved from a single block of wood or alternatively built in sections like the staved back of a full size instrument. Again, the tuning follows the traditional 3-course Greek long necked lute family, utilizing the modal D-A-D setup.

Musically, the tzouras uses the lower third course of strings as a drone, while the top two courses (strings 1-4) play the melody.

Waldzither (*or* Forest Zither)

A traditional German 9-string/5-course cittern tuned to an open C chord (CGCEG) and featuring a scale length of between 430mm and 460mm. Two distinct styles exist - the first being the earlier Thüringen instrument with its regular mandolin/guitar style tuners. The second being a later 1900 design patented by German company C. H. Böhm with its drum/piano key-style tuners, which closely resemble the watch-key tuners used on the Portuguese guitar.

The most popular member of the Waldzither family is the tenor, but other sizes also exist including the piccolo (an octave higher, also tuned CGCEG), the descant or *diskant* (tuned GDGBD) and the bass (AEAC#E). An alternative tuning for the tenor features an open D Major chord (DADF#A) - a whole tone higher than the standard open C.

Mandolin Family Tunings

The following list of cittern and mandolin family members includes a selection of some of the more widely used standard and popular tunings. The tuning arrangement in the right hand column lists the notes from right to left (or low to high).

Instrument	Tuning
Baglama	DAD
Bandolim	GDAE
Bandurria	G#C#F#BEA
Bouzouki - Tetrachordo Tuning	CFAD
Bouzouki - Tetrachordo *Guitar* Tuning	DGBE
Bouzouki - Trichordo Tuning	DAD
Bouzouki - Trichordo Alternate Tuning	EBE
Cittern (Longscale Fifths Tuning)	CGDAE
Cittern (Longscale Irish Tuning)	DGDAD
Cittern (Longscale Mandocello+Tuning)	CGDAD
Cittern (Longscale Mandolin+Tuning)	DGDAE
Cittern (Longscale Modal A Tuning)	EAEAE
Cittern (Longscale Modal C Tuning)	CGCGC
Cittern (Longscale Modal D Tuning)	DADAD
Cittern (Longscale Modal F Tuning)	CFCFC
Cittern (Longscale Modal G Tuning)	DGDGD
Cittern (Longscale Asus4 Tuning)	DAEAE
Cittern (Shortscale Fifths Tuning)	GDAEB
Cittern (Shortscale Mandolin+Tuning)	GDAEA
Cittern (Shortscale Modal C Tuning)	GCGCG
Cittern (Shortscale Modal D Tuning)	ADADA
Cittern (Shortscale Modal F Tuning)	FCFCF
Cittern (Shortscale Modal G Tuning)	GDGDG
Cittern (Shortscale Dsus4 Tuning)	GDADA
English Guittar *or* English Guitar	CEGCEG
Greek Bouzouki	CFAD
Halszither (Krienser)	GDGBD
Halszither (Toggenburger)	CGCEG
Harzzither	GCEG
Irish Bouzouki (Fifths Tuning)	GDAE
Irish Bouzouki (Irish Tuning)	GDAD
Irish Bouzouki (Modal D Tuning)	ADAD
Irish Bouzouki (Modal G Tuning)	GDGD
Laúd (Cuban Tuning)	DF#BEAD
Laúd (Filipino Tuning)	F#BEADG
Laúd (Spanish Tuning)	G#C#F#BEA
Mandobass	EADG
Mandocello	GCDA
Mandola *or* Tenor Mandola	CGDA
Mandolin	GDAE
Octave Mandolin *or* Octave Mandola	GDAE
Piccolo or Soprano Mandolin	CGDA
Portuguese Guitar (Coimbra Tuning)	CGADGA
Portuguese Guitar (Lisboa Tuning)	DABEAB
Portuguese Guitar (Natural Tuning)	CEGCEG
Tambura - Bulgarian	DGBE
Tambura Cello - Bulgarian	DGBE
Tambura Pirin - Bulgarian	DAD
Tamburitza Berda/Bas	EADG
Tamburitza Bugarija	GBDG
Tamburitza Brač	EADG
Tamburitza Čelo & Čelović	EADG
Tamburitza Prim & Bisernica	EADG
Tricordia *or* Mandriola	GDAE
Tzouras	DAD
Waldzither (Bass in A Major)	AEAC#E
Waldzither (Descant in G Major)	GDGBD
Waldzither (Piccolo in C Major)	CGCEG
Waldzither (Tenor in Standard C Major)	CGCEG
Waldzither (Tenor in D Major)	DADF#A

ALTERNATIVE CHORD NAMES

C	**CM** or **Cmaj**	Cm13	**C-13** or **Cmin13**
Cm	**Cmin** or **C-**	Cmaj13	**CM13, Cmaj7(add13),**
C-5	**C-5** or **C(♭5)**		**C△13** or **CM7(add13)**
C°	**Cdim**		
C4	**Csus4(no 5th)** or **Csus(no 5th)**		
C5	**C Power Chord** or **C(no 3rd)**		
Csus2	**C(sus2)** or **C2**		
Csus4	**Csus** or **C(sus4)**		
Csus4add9	**Csus(add9)**		
C+	**Caug, C+5** or **C(♯5)**		
C6	**CM6** or **CMaj6**		
Cadd9	**Cadd2**		
Cm6	**C-6** or **Cmin6**		
Cmadd9	**Cmadd2** or **C-(add9)**		
C6add9	**C6/9, C⁶₉** or **CMaj6(add9)**		
Cm6add9	**Cm6/9** or **Cm⁶₉**		
C°7	**Cdim7**		
C7	**Cdom**		
C7sus2	**C7(sus2)**		
C7sus4	**C7sus, C7(sus4)** or **Csus11**		
C7-5	**C7♭5**		
C7+5	**C7+** or **C7♯5**		
C7-9	**C7♭9** or **C7(add♭9)**		
C7+9	**C7♯9** or **C7(add♯9)**		
C7-5-9	**C7♭5♭9**		
C7+5-9	**C7♯5♭9**		
C7+5+9	**C7♯5♯9**		
C7add11	**C7/11** or **C⁷₁₁**		
C7+11	**C7♯11**		
Cm7	**C-7, Cmi7** or **Cmin7**		
Cm7-5	**Cm7♭5, C-7-5** or **C⌀**		
Cm7-5-9	**Cm7♭5♭9**		
Cm7-9	**Cm7♭9**		
Cm7add11	**Cm**		
Cm(maj7)	**Cm♯7, CM7-5, CmM7** or **C-△**		
Cmaj7	**CM7** or **C△(Delta)**		
Cmaj7-5	**CM7-5, C△♭5** or **Cmaj7♭5**		
Cmaj7+5	**CM7+5, C△5+** or **Cmaj7♯11**		
Cmaj7+11	**CM7+11, C△+♯11** or **Cmaj7♯11**		
C9	**C7(add9)**		
C9sus4	**C9sus** or **C9(sus4)**		
C9-5	**C9♭5**		
C9+5	**C9♯5**		
C9+11	**C9♯11**		
Cm9	**C-9** or **Cmin9**		
Cm9-5	**Cm9♭5**		
Cm(maj9)	**Cm9(maj7), CmM9** or **Cm(addM9)**		
Cmaj9	**CM9, Cmaj7(add9), C△9** or **CM7(add9)**		
Cmaj9-5	**CM9-5, Cmaj9♭5, C△9♭5** or **CM9♭5**		
Cmaj9+5	**CM9+5, Cmaj9♯5, C△9♯5**		
Cmaj9add6	**CM9add6** or **C△9add6**		
Cmaj9+11	**CM9+11, Cmaj9♯11, C△9♯11** or **CM9♯11**		
C11	**C7(add11)**		
C11-9	**C11♭9**		
Cm11	**C-11** or **Cmin11**		
Cmaj11	**CM11, Cmaj7(add11), C△11, CM7(add11)**		
C13	**C7/6(no 9th)** or **C7(add13)**		
C13sus4	**C13sus** or **C13(sus4)**		
C13-5-9	**C13♭5♭9**		
C13-9	**C13♭9**		
C13+9	**C13♯9**		
C13+11	**C13♯11** or **C13aug11**		

M	**major**
m	**minor**
-	**minor**
dim	**diminished**
°	**diminished**
⌀	**half diminished**
sus	**suspended**
aug	**augmented**
+	**augmented**
add	**added**
dom	**dominant**
△	**delta / major seventh**
Q(3)	**quartal / double fourth**
♯	**sharp**
×	**double sharp**
♭	**flat**
♭♭	**double flat**

Do	**Spanish for C**
Dó	**Portuguese for C**
Re	**Spanish for D**
Ré	**Portuguese for D**
Mi	**Spanish & Portuguese for E**
Fa	**Spanish & Portuguese for F**
So	**Spanish for G**
Sol	**Portuguese for G**
La	**Spanish for A**
Lá	**Portuguese for A**
Si	**Spanish & Portuguese for B**
H	**German for B**

English Tonic Sol-fa

Do	**C**
Re	**D**
Me	**E**
Fa	**F**
Sol	**G**
La	**A**
Ti	**B**

The majority of music books will use the chords featured in the first column (on the far left and top right), but should you come across alternatives, consult this guide for other naming conventions.

The list above includes most of the symbols and abbreviations that you're likely to encounter in the majority of music books.

NOTES

NOTES

NOTES

www.ingramcontent.com/pod-product-compliance
Lightning Source LLC
Chambersburg PA
CBHW081119080526
44587CB00021B/3664